KNOWING GOD'S WILL

A 4-week course to help Christian teenagers understand what it means to seek and follow God's will

by Cindy S. Hansen

Group®
Loveland, Colorado

Knowing God's Will

Credits
Edited by Stephen Parolini
Cover designed by Jill Bendykowski and DeWain Stoll
Interior designed by Judy Atwood Bienick and Jan Aufdemberge
Illustrations by Roseanne Buerge
Cover photo by David Priest and Brenda Rundback
Photo on p. 26 by Rick Whitmer

Scripture quotations are from the Holy Bible, New International Version. Copyright © 1973, 1978, 1984 International Bible Society. Used by permission of Zondervan Bible Publishers.

ISBN 1-55945-205-6
Printed in the United States of America

CONTENTS

KNOWING GOD'S WILL

"Should I go to college after I graduate?"
"What should I say to my friend who wants me to go with her to a drinking party?"
"Is it okay to have sex with someone you love?"
"What will I be doing five years from now?"
"Should I become a pastor or a missionary?"

● ● ●

Teenagers today want to know answers to a lot of different questions: questions about the future, questions of right or wrong, and questions about day-to-day issues.

Witness the top interests of teenagers today from a survey of Christian teenagers.

Kids today are most interested in:

1. making friends and knowing how to be a friend

2. learning to know and love Jesus

3. learning more about who God is

4. learning to love life more

5. recognizing right and wrong, and making good decisions

Kids will probably face tough decisions in each of these areas as they grow into adulthood. Is it okay to take drugs? How should I respond to the homeless or world hunger? How should I relate to my non-Christian friends?

Teenagers need guidance in each of these decisions. But often they don't know where to find that guidance. When kids pray "your will be done" in the Lord's Prayer, they're right on track for finding the answers. Knowing God's will helps kids make good decisions about their future, moral issues and even day-to-day concerns.

But many kids don't know how to discover God's will for their lives. They see God's will as something in the future—something yet to be discovered about their life's vocation.

This course will help teenagers see how God's will is something "now" as well as future. It'll give them concrete methods for discovering God's will. Teenagers will learn how to seek God's will for little, everyday decisions as well as major, potentially life-changing decisions. They'll learn how to consider God's will for questions of right or wrong. They'll learn how to accept God's forgiveness when they make bad decisions—and how to focus once again on doing God's will.

Help kids find guidance for tough questions.

Help kids discover and live out God's will for their lives.

HOW TO USE THIS COURSE

Think back on an important lesson you've learned in life. Did you learn it from reading about it? from hearing about it? from something you experienced? Chances are, the most important lessons you've learned came from something you experienced. That's what active learning is—learning by doing. And active learning is a key element in Group's Active Bible Curriculum.

Active learning leads students in doing things that help them understand important principles, messages and ideas. It's a discovery process that helps kids internalize what they learn.

Each lesson section in Group's Active Bible Curriculum plays an important part in active learning:

The **Opener** involves kids in the topic in fun and unusual ways.

The **Action and Reflection** includes an experience designed to evoke specific feelings in the students. This section also processes those feelings through "How did you feel?" questions and applies the message to situations kids face.

The **Bible Application** actively connects the topic with the Bible. It helps kids see how the Bible is relevant to the situations they face.

The **Commitment** helps students internalize the Bible's message and commit to make changes in their lives.

The **Closing** funnels the lesson's message into a time of creative reflection and prayer.

When you put all the sections together, you get a lesson that's fun to teach—and kids get messages they'll remember.

● Read the Introduction, the Course Objectives and This Course at a Glance (p. 8).

● Decide how you'll publicize the course using the art on the Publicity Page (p. 9). Prepare fliers, newsletter articles and posters as needed.

● Look at the Bonus Ideas (p. 41) and decide which ones you'll use.

● Read the opening statements, Objectives and Bible Basis for the lesson. The Bible Basis shows how specific passages relate to senior highers today.

● Choose which Opener and Closing options to use. Each is appropriate for a different kind of group. The first option is often more active.

● Gather necessary supplies from This Lesson at a Glance.

● Read each section of the lesson. Adjust where necessary for your class size and meeting room.

● The approximate minutes listed give you an idea of how long each activity will take. Each lesson is designed to take 35 to 60 minutes. Shorten or lengthen activities as needed to fit your group.

● If you see you're going to have extra time, do an activity or two from the "If You Still Have Time . . . " box or from the Bonus Ideas (p. 41).

● Dive into the activities with the kids. Don't be a spectator. The lesson will be more successful and rewarding to both you and your students.

● The answers given after discussion questions are responses your students *might* give. They aren't the only answers or the "right" answers. If needed, use them to spark discussion. Kids won't always say what you wish they'd say. That's why some of the responses given are negative or controversial. If someone responds negatively, don't be shocked. Accept the person, and use the opportunity to explore other angles of the issue.

COURSE OBJECTIVES

By the end of this course your students will:
- learn that God gives us prayer, others, the Bible and the church to help discover his will;
- commit to use the ways God gives them to know his will;
- discover how they can use their abilities to follow God's will;
- think of ways to do God's will in their daily lives;
- chart their goals for five, 10 and 15 years from now;
- accept God's forgiveness for the times they've messed up; and
- celebrate God's forgiveness.

THIS COURSE AT A GLANCE

Before you dive into the lessons, familiarize yourself with each lesson aim. Then read the scripture passages.
- Study them as a background to the lessons.
- Use them as a basis for your personal devotions.
- Think about how they relate to teenagers' circumstances today.

LESSON 1: HOW DO I KNOW GOD'S WILL?
Lesson Aim: To show senior highers that God has given us several ways to help us know his will.
Bible Basis: Jeremiah 29:11-13 and Matthew 5:1-12.

LESSON 2: DOING GOD'S WILL
Lesson Aim: To show senior highers they can use their abilities to do God's will with their hearts, souls, bodies and minds.
Bible Basis: Matthew 22:37-40 and Galatians 5:13-15.

LESSON 3: CHARTING YOUR FUTURE
Lesson Aim: To show teenagers that God is interested in their future and can help them as they follow him.
Bible Basis: Proverbs 3:5-6; Proverbs 16:3-4a; and Isaiah 41:10.

LESSON 4: WHEN YOU'VE MESSED UP
Lesson Aim: To help kids accept God's forgiveness when they've messed up.
Bible Basis: Luke 15:11-32 and Philippians 3:13.

PUBLICITY PAGE

Grab your senior highers' attention! Copy this page, then cut and paste the art of your choice in your church bulletin or newsletter to advertise this course on knowing God's will. Or copy and use the ready-made flier as a bulletin insert.

Splash this art on posters, fliers or even postcards! Just add the vital details: the date and time the course begins, and where you'll meet.

It's that simple.

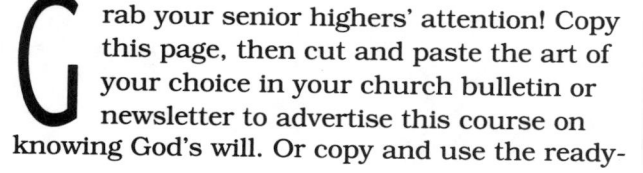

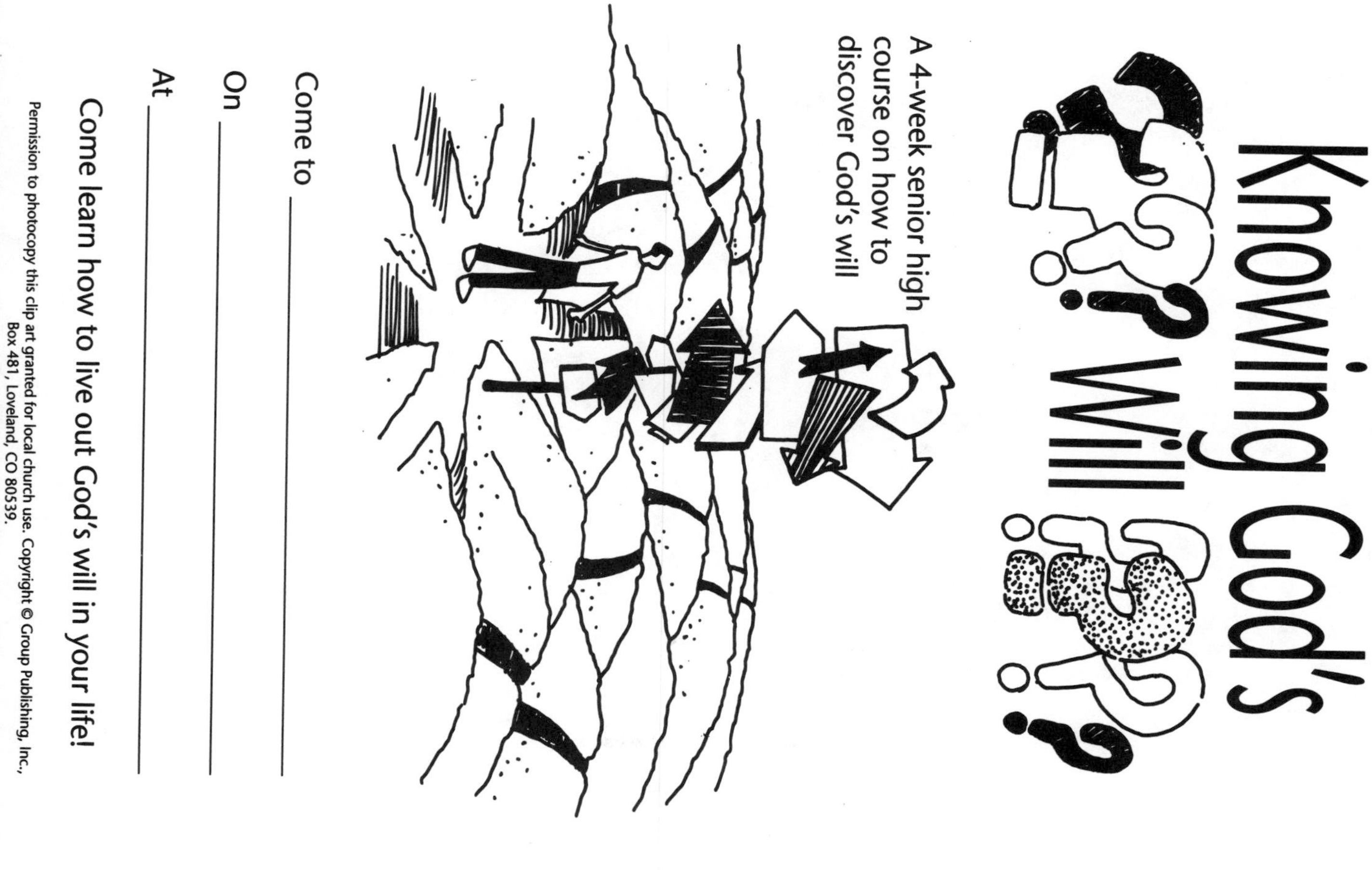

A 4-week senior high course on how to discover God's will

Come to _____

On _____

At _____

Come learn how to live out God's will in your life!

HOW DO I KNOW GOD'S WILL?

Many teenagers desire to follow God but don't know how. They hear "just follow God's will" but don't really know what that means. God didn't leave us alone to just guess at what he wants for us. Kids can find help in seeking God's will for their lives.

LESSON AIM

To show senior highers that God has given us several ways to help us know his will.

OBJECTIVES

Students will:
- experience what it's like to have difficulty finding something;
- discover some of God's "wills" and "won'ts" for their lives;
- learn that God gives us prayer, others, his Word and the church to help discover his will; and
- commit to use the ways God gives us to know his will.

BIBLE BASIS
JEREMIAH 29:11-13
MATTHEW 5:1-12

Look up the following scriptures. Then read the background paragraphs to see how the passages relate to your senior highers.

In **Jeremiah 29:11-13**, God tells the captives in Bablyon that he has a plan for them.

This passage gave Jeremiah and the exiles encouragement in a tough time. God told the exiles through Jeremiah that his plan for them was going to be good. He also promised that if people really sought God, they'd find him.

Senior highers today hear conflicting advice from many different sources. They sometimes have trouble knowing what God would have them do. This passage can assure them that God has not deserted them! He'll let them know what he wants them to do if they seek him sincerely.

In **Matthew 5:1-11**, Jesus gives us guidelines for living. This passage—often called the Beatitudes—gives us general principles that can apply to many situations in everyday living. Some topics that concern us aren't specifically addressed in scripture. But many times the qualities in this passage—such as humility, righteousness and mercy—can guide us in making decisions on tough issues.

This passage can help senior highers see a glimpse of God's will for their lives. The passage is one of many provided by God for helping us understand his will.

THIS LESSON AT A GLANCE

Section	Minutes	What Students Will Do	Supplies
Opener (Option 1)	5 to 10	**Blind Search**—Play a game that illustrates "blindly searching" for God's will.	Blindfold
(Option 2)		**Blind Scripture Search**—See how a blindfolded person struggles to find a Bible.	Bible, blindfold
Action and Reflection	10 to 15	**God's Will or Won't?**—Make collages showing what God wants and doesn't want.	Magazines, newsprint, glue or tape
Bible Application	15 to 20	**Ways to God's Will**—Complete a handout and learn ways to seek God's will.	"This Way to God's Will!" handouts (p. 17), pencils
Commitment	5 to 10	**Fitting It All Together**—Write what they'll do to seek God's will.	"God's Will Puzzle" handouts (p. 18), scissors, pencils, envelopes
Closing (Option 1)	up to 5	**Thanks to God**—Pray a responsive prayer, thanking God for his guidance.	
(Option 2)		**Unpuzzled Circle**—Circle around completed puzzles and pray.	Puzzles from Fitting It All Together

The Lesson

OPENER
(5 to 10 minutes)

OPTION 1: BLIND SEARCH

Begin by choosing one senior higher to be your searcher. Blindfold that person and have him or her stand in the middle of the room. Have the other kids scatter around the edges of the room, each standing an arm's length away from any other person—if that's possible in your classroom.

Once kids are in their places, instruct them to not move their feet and to remain absolutely quiet. Then spin your searcher around three times, and tell him or her to take five steps forward. If the searcher touches someone, that person trades places with the searcher. If not, give the searcher a few more spins in that spot and let him or her try again. Keep going until at least four or five kids have had a chance to be the searcher.

Ask:

● **How did it feel to be the searcher?** (Frustrating; confusing.)

● **When have you felt that way in real life?**

● **How is that kind of searching like searching for God's will in your life?** (We don't have much guidance; sometimes I think I should just close my eyes and point to a choice.)

Say: **Sometimes it seems like we're groping blindly when we search for God's will. But today we're going to look at some ways we can find what God wants for our lives.**

OPTION 2: BLIND SCRIPTURE SEARCH

Begin by sending one teenager out of the room while you give directions to the other kids. Place a Bible at some out-of-the-way place in the room. Then form three groups. Tell one group to shout directions that would lead the searcher away from the Bible. Tell another group to shout random directions, some toward the Bible and some away from it. Tell the third group to shout directions toward the Bible. Tell kids they can only use the following directional commands: "forward," "backward," "right," "left," "up" and "down."

Then blindfold your searcher, bring him or her back into the room and signal the kids to start shouting their directions.

Afterward, ask:

● **How did it feel to be the searcher?** (Frustrating; confusing.)

● **When have you felt that way in real life?**

● **How is that kind of searching like searching for God's will in your life?** (Everyone tells me something different to do; I can't tell which decision is right.)

Say: **Sometimes it seems really confusing when we search for God's will. But today we're going to look at some ways we can find what God wants for our lives.**

GOD'S WILL OR WON'T?

Form pairs. Distribute to each pair an assortment of magazines, a sheet of newsprint, and glue or transparent tape. Have pairs each turn their newsprint horizontally and label one side of the paper "God's Will" and the other side "God's Won't."

ACTION AND REFLECTION
(10 to 15 minutes)

Allow five minutes for pairs each to tear pictures and words from the magazines and attach them to the newsprint under the appropriate heading. Under "God's Will" they might put smiles, sunshine or people helping other people. Under "God's Won't" they might put drugs, people starving or people hurting other people.

Ask:

● **What made you put certain things under one heading and others under another?** (I know God likes those things; the Bible says we should help people.)

● **How do we know what God wants for us and what he doesn't want for us?** (We study the Bible; we listen to what our pastor says; we pray and see if God makes things happen.)

WAYS TO GOD'S WILL

Say: **It's not always easy to know exactly what God wants for us. Some things are clearly spelled out for us in the Bible while others aren't. But even with the tough decisions, God has given us ways to help decide what he would have us choose.**

Distribute the "This Way to God's Will!" handouts (p. 17) and pencils. Form four groups. A group can be one person. Assign one section of the handout to each group, and have groups each read their scriptures and answer the questions related to their topic. Then have groups report their findings to the rest of the class while class members each fill in answers on their handout.

When the groups have reported, ask volunteers to share how God has helped them make a decision using at least one of the ways you've just talked about. Have a life experience of your own ready to share as a starter.

FITTING IT ALL TOGETHER

Say: **We've seen ways that can help us discover God's will for us. Now let's decide what we're really going to do.**

Before class, photocopy and cut apart a puzzle for each student from the "God's Will Puzzle" handout (p. 18). Put each cut-up puzzle in a separate envelope.

Pass out pencils and the envelopes with the puzzle pieces. Have kids each write on each puzzle piece how they'll use that element when they're puzzled about God's will for them. For example, for prayer someone might write, "I will pray and open myself to God's answers and direction." For the church, someone might write, "I'll ask my Sunday school teacher for advice, and I'll soak up all the support I can from other Christians."

When kids have finished writing on their puzzle pieces, instruct them each to put the pieces together to form a square. When they're finished, say: **When we use all the methods**

BIBLE APPLICATION
(15 to 20 minutes)

COMMITMENT
(5 to 10 minutes)

God has given us to seek his will, things will often fit together like the pieces of a puzzle. Even when it doesn't seem like there's a way, God can work it out.

Form pairs. Have teenagers each briefly share their completed puzzle and then say one thing they appreciate about the ideas their partner wrote on their puzzle.

Encourage kids to take their puzzles home to remind them of what they said they'd do in seeking God's will.

Table Talk

The Table Talk activity in this course helps senior highers discuss with their parents how to know and live out God's will.

If you choose to use the Table Talk activity, this is a good time to show students the "Table Talk" handout (p. 19). Ask them to spend time with their parents completing it.

Before kids leave, give them each the "Table Talk" handout to take home, or tell them you'll be sending it to their parents.

Or use the Table Talk idea found in the Bonus Ideas (p. 42) for a meeting based on the handout.

CLOSING
(up to 5 minutes)

OPTION 1: THANKS TO GOD!

Pray a responsive prayer, thanking God for his guidance. After you say each incomplete sentence, have kids finish it with the words "prayer, others, the Bible and the church."

Leader: God, we thank you for showing us your will for our lives through ...

Kids: prayer, others, the Bible and the church.

Leader: When we question what's best for us at school or at home, help us to seek you through ...

Kids: prayer, others, the Bible and the church.

Leader: When we question what's best for us in our relationships and our lives, help us to seek you through ...

Kids: prayer, others, the Bible and the church.

Leader: Amen.

OPTION 2: UNPUZZLED CIRCLE

Form an "unpuzzled" circle by having kids arrange their assembled puzzles from Fitting It All Together in a circle on the floor. Then have the teenagers gather around the circle of puzzles and link arms. Pray together asking God to help all of you remember to use prayer, others, the Bible and the church when searching for God's will in your lives. Encourage kids to take their puzzles home with them to remind them of what they said they'd do in seeking God's will.

If You Still Have Time . . .

God's Will or Not?—Write several things each on a separate 3×5 card that might be questionable in relation to God's will—drinking, smoking, using drugs, dancing, lying to protect a friend from injury, making out, abortion, AIDS, war. As a group, have kids decide which ones are definitely God's will, which are definitely not God's will and which they're not certain about.

Have kids give their reasoning for each choice. Discuss what kinds of input—prayer, the Bible, others or the church—might be most helpful in deciding on the uncertain ones.

How Others Found It—Have kids do a study of how Bible characters discovered God's will for their lives. You might want to include these scriptures: Judges 6:36-40; 1 Samuel 16:1-13; Matthew 4:17-22; and Acts 11:19-24.

THIS WAY TO
Gods Will!

Read through the passages for your topic and answer the questions related to them.

Prayer—Jeremiah 29:11-13; 1 Thessalonians 5:16-18; and James 1:4-6.
- How does prayer help you know God's will for your life?

- List four decisions you're facing in which prayer might help you make the right choice.

_____

_____

_____

_____

The Bible—Exodus 20:1-17; Matthew 5:1-12; and 2 Timothy 3:16-17.
- How does the Bible help you know God's will for your life?

- List four decisions you're facing in which the Bible might help you make the right choice.

_____

_____

_____

_____

Others—Proverbs 6:20-23; Proverbs 11:11-14; and 1 Thessalonians 5:11-14.
- How do others help you know God's will for your life?

- List four decisions you're facing in which other people might help you make the right choice.

_____

_____

_____

_____

The Church—Acts 13:1-3; 2 Thessalonians 1:1-12; and 1 Peter 4:7-11.
- How does the church help you know God's will for your life?

- List four decisions you're facing in which the church might help you make the right choice.

_____

_____

_____

_____

GOD'S WILL
PUZZLE

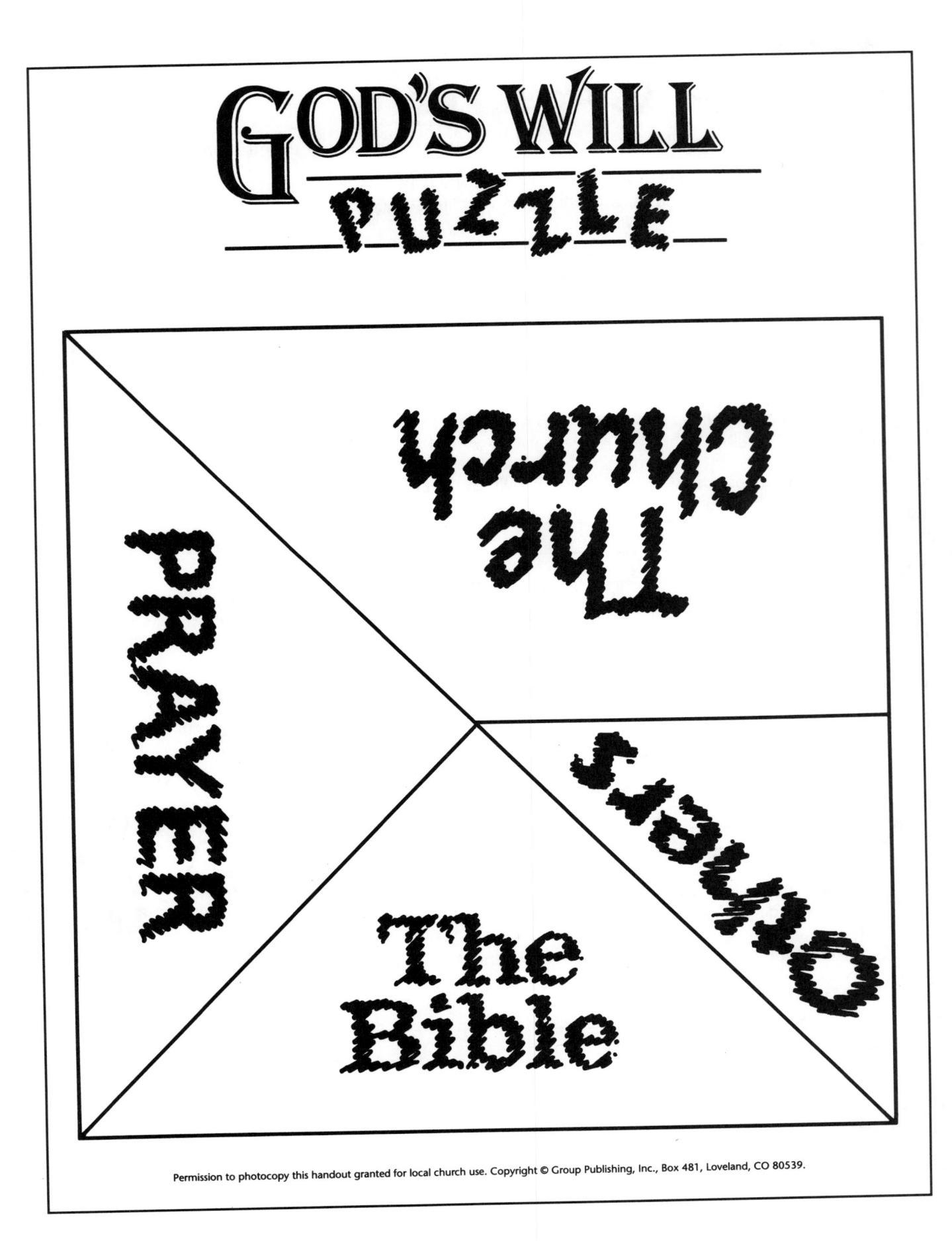

PRAYER

The Church

Others

The Bible

Table Talk

To the Parent: We're involved in a senior high course at church called Knowing God's Will. Students are learning how to know and live out God's will for their lives. We'd like you and your teenager to spend some time discussing this important topic. Use this sheet to help you do that.

Parent and teenager

Take turns describing how you know what God wants you to do with your life. Also describe how you know what God doesn't want you to do.

Parent

Tell of a recent problem you had at work or with a friend.
● How'd you know what God wanted you to do in that situation?
● Would you have handled it differently if you could've talked to other people or spent time praying and studying the Bible before you responded?

Teenager

Tell of a recent problem you had at school.
● How did you know what God wanted you to do in that situation?
● Would you have handled it differently if you could've talked to other people or spent time praying and studying the Bible before you responded?

Parent and teenager

Take turns asking "What would you do if...?" situations. For example, "Mom, what would you do if you found out a friend was spreading a bad rumor about you?" Include ways you'd seek God's will in each situation.

Teenager

Share what you wrote on your puzzle pieces about how you would seek God's will.

Parent and teenager

Discuss how you can help each other in seeking God's will for your lives.

Then read together the following scripture. Talk about how it can help you as you seek to do God's will:

"Be very careful, then, how you live—not as unwise but as wise, making the most of every opportunity, because the days are evil. Therefore do not be foolish, but understand what the Lord's will is" (Ephesians 5:15-17).

DOING GOD'S WILL

Part of knowing God's will for the future involves following what we know as his will for our daily lives. And one thing we know is that we're to follow him completely—with our hearts, souls, bodies and minds. As teenagers learn to follow God in little things daily, they'll be ready to follow him when big decisions come along.

LESSON AIM

To show senior highers they can use their abilities to do God's will with their hearts, souls, bodies and minds.

OBJECTIVES

Students will:
- **examine what different actions relate to doing God's will with their heart, soul, body or mind;**
- **discover how they can use their abilities to follow God's will;**
- **think of ways to do God's will in their daily lives; and**
- **commit to doing God's will in a specific way.**

BIBLE BASIS
MATTHEW 22:37-40
GALATIANS 5:13-15

Look up the following scriptures. Then read the background paragraphs to see how the passages relate to your senior highers.

In **Matthew 22:37-40**, Jesus describes the greatest commandment.

This passage lets us know what's important to God: He wants us to follow him with every part of our being. That means we should follow him in every little daily decision, not just wait for the big ones to come along and then ask for help.

Senior highers need to know that God *does* want them to follow him in their daily lives. He's not just a God for Sunday or for youth group. He's a God that wants his people to follow him every minute of their lives.

In **Galatians 5:13-15**, Paul explains what's most important to God.

In this passage we read that we're called to be free. But this freedom does not mean "do as you like" for Christians. Paul sums up the law in "Love your neighbor as you love yourself." This was similar to Jesus' answer to the Pharisees' question about the greatest commandment.

Loving the Lord with heart, soul, body and mind, and loving your neighbor as yourself are the "prime directives" of God's will for Christians. And senior highers are ready to begin using their abilities to follow these directives.

THIS LESSON AT A GLANCE

Section	Minutes	What Students Will Do	Supplies
Opener (Option 1)	5 to 10	**Shaping Time**—Mold something from materials supplied.	Popsicle sticks, rubber bands, aluminum foil
(Option 2)		**Shapes in Silence**—Hold a piece of clay or make something from it.	Modeling clay
Action and Reflection	10 to 15	**Heart, Soul, Body and Mind**—Play a game using the ideas from God's most important commandment.	
Bible Application	10 to 15	**Doing It**—Think of ways to use their abilities to follow God's will.	"Doing God's Will" handouts (p. 26), pencils, Bibles
Commitment	10 to 15	**Getting Started**—Choose a way to follow God this week.	Newsprint, marker, 3×5 cards, pencils
Closing (Option 1)	up to 5	**God's Will-O-Grams**—Make an acrostic from their name listing ways to do God's will.	Paper, pencils
(Option 2)		**Asking for Help**—Pray that God will help them do what they've committed to do.	

The Lesson

OPTION 1: SHAPING TIME

Give each student four popsicle sticks, four rubber bands and a square sheet of aluminum foil. Tell kids each to create something from what you've given them. When kids are finished, have them display and explain their creations.

OPENER
(5 to 10 minutes)

Say: **Notice that no two creations are exactly alike. That's the way it is with humans too—no two people are exactly alike. God wants the best for each of us, but that may be different for each person. Today we're going to explore what it means for each of us to do God's will.**

OPTION 2: SHAPES IN SILENCE

As students arrive, give each a lump of modeling clay, but don't give the students any directions. Then go on with your normal opening conversation or simply spend three or four minutes talking about how everyone's doing.

Ask:

● **What did you do with your clay?**

● **How is what you did with your clay like the way some people follow God's will?** (Some people don't do anything with God's will; everybody does it differently.)

Say: **You didn't all do the same thing with your clay, and that's okay. That's like the way it is with our lives. God wants each of us to do something different with our lives. Today we're going to look at what it means for each of us to do God's will.**

Table Talk Follow-Up

If you sent the "Table Talk" handout (p. 19) to parents last week, discuss students' reactions to the activity. Ask volunteers to share what they learned from the discussion with their parents.

ACTION AND REFLECTION

(10 to 15 minutes)

HEART, SOUL, BODY AND MIND

Ask:

● **When we search for God's will by reading the Bible, listening to others or praying, what do we hope to discover?** (What we should do in the future; what we should do in specific situations.)

● **Does God's will just relate to our future? Explain.** (Yes, God's will is what we should do with our lives; no, God's will involves day-to-day decisions too.)

Say: **Some parts of God's will are very clear to us from the Bible. And these parts of God's will affect our day-to-day choices. According to the Bible, God wants each of us to love him with our heart, soul, body and mind. And he wants us to love our neighbors as ourselves.**

Have teenagers stand in a circle.

Say: **I'm going to read some actions that may be part of doing God's will. If you think an action is related to the heart or emotions, point to your heart. If you think it's** related to the soul or spiritual nature, point to the sole of your shoe. If you think it's related to the body or physical nature, flex your arm to make a muscle. If you think it's related to the mind or intellect, point to your brain.

Read the actions from the box in the margin and let kids point. Many of the actions could relate to two or more choices.

Ask:

● **What did you notice about the way people responded to each item?** (Some people had different responses; most of the responses were the same.)

● **How can God's desire for us to love him with our heart, soul, body and mind affect our choices in the situations we just listed?** (If we love God with our mind, we'll work harder in school; if we love God with our soul, we'll search for new understanding of him and grow in faith.)

Say: **We sometimes choose to do negative things with our hearts, souls, bodies and minds. Let's think about what some of those might be.**

Have your kids brainstorm some actions for each category: heart, soul, body and mind; for example: telling someone you hate him or her, denying your faith when talking to a friend, taking drugs and ignoring school assignments. Then say: **When we concentrate on loving God with our heart, soul, body and mind, and learn to love others as ourselves, we'll more easily be able to avoid those actions that aren't God's will. Now let's think of some of the good actions we might do in following what we know is God's will.**

Let kids brainstorm good actions for each category: heart, soul, body and mind; for example: helping a neighbor, praying daily, exercising regularly and studying for tests.

Ask:

● **How is doing these good actions the same as following God's will?** (God wants us to please him with our actions; God's will for us is to serve him.)

Then say: **God has given us gifts and abilities to help us do those things that make up his will for us. Let's take a look at some of those gifts and abilities.**

Heart, Soul, Body or Mind?
● forgiving a friend
● going to church
● refusing to take illegal drugs
● deciding to go to college
● helping a brother or sister with homework
● eating healthy foods and exercising
● refusing to repeat gossip
● gathering food to give to the homeless
● trusting in Christ as your Savior

DOING IT

Distribute copies of the "Doing God's Will" handout (p. 26). Have kids each fill out their handout.

When they're finished, have kids share their ideas for doing God's will. Then have someone read aloud Galatians 5:13-14.

Ask:

● **How does this verse describe doing God's will?** (To serve each other with love; not to be selfish.)

BIBLE APPLICATION
(10 to 15 minutes)

● **What warning does this passage give us about not following God's will?** (We'll end up hurting each other; we'll destroy each other.)

COMMITMENT
(10 to 15 minutes)

GETTING STARTED

Say: **God wants us to follow him with all of our being—with our heart, soul, body and mind. And there are lots of ways to do that. Let's brainstorm some we haven't mentioned already.**

Have someone from your group list the ideas on newsprint as they're suggested. Ask teenagers to be specific. Be sure no ideas are criticized.

After you have 10 or more new ideas listed, pass out 3×5 cards and pencils.

Say: **Now choose a way you're going to follow God's will this week. It can be one of these or one we talked about earlier. Write a brief description on one side of the card of what you're going to do. Someone else will be reading your card.**

Allow a minute for kids to write, then form pairs. Say: **Now turn your card over and write a brief note congratulating your partner for how you've seen him or her following God's will in his or her life. For example, you could write, "Congratulations, Chris! You do God's will in your life by being friendly and making everyone feel welcome." After you've written the note, give the card to your partner.**

After pairs have shared their congratulations, have them talk about what they wrote on the other side of the card and agree to pray for each other about what they'll do to follow God's will. Encourage partners to check with each other in the following weeks to see how each other is doing.

CLOSING
(up to 5 minutes)

OPTION 1: GOD'S-WILL-O-GRAMS

Give kids paper and pencils. Have kids each write an acrostic using their name and ideas for doing God's will. Here's an example for the name Abby:

Always listen and
Be willing to treat others as you would like to
Be treated.
You should remember to love God with all your heart, body and mind.

Have kids read aloud their God's-Will-O-Grams. Then close with prayer that God will help your kids do what they committed to do in following God's will in their lives.

OPTION 2: ASKING FOR HELP

Say: **God never asks us to do something we're incapable of doing. However, we often do need his help in following** his will. So let's pray together asking God to help us do the things we've committed to do. As we pray, ask God to help you specifically with what you chose to do. If you wrote on your card that you'd quit squabbling with your sister, tell God that and ask him to help you with it.

Give time for volunteers to pray aloud, then wrap up the class with your own prayer, also telling what you committed to do.

If You Still Have Time . . .

Heart-Soul-Body-and-Mind Mobiles—Pass out construction paper to your senior highers and form four groups: the heart group, the soul group, the body group and the mind group. Have kids each tear something out of their construction paper to symbolize their group. Then have them write on their symbol one thing that's part of doing God's will in relation to their group's topic. Have them use string and wire hangers to make a mobile from the symbols. Display the mobile for the rest of the class sessions.

Steps to God's Will—Lay a large sheet of newsprint or butcher paper on the floor. Have kids each trace their feet—all going the same direction—on the paper. Then have kids write in their own footprints ways they can follow God's will in their lives daily. Tape the paper to the wall as a reminder.

Doing God's Will

1. Think about the gifts and abilities God has given you. List at least five below; for example: good student, friendly, athletic.

2. Read Matthew 22:37-40. Jesus says we should love him with all our heart. What are ways you can use your abilities and gifts? Write your ideas below; for example: look for new kids who're struggling and be their friend.

3. Jesus says to love him with all our soul. What are ways you can use your abilities and gifts? Write your ideas below; for example: invite a friend to a Bible study or youth group.

4. Paul taught that we should honor God with our bodies. What are ways you can use your abilities and gifts? Write your ideas below; for example: avoid drugs so I can have a healthy body.

5. Jesus says to love him with all our mind. What are ways you can use your abilities and gifts? Write your ideas below; for example: be the best student I can be.

6. Jesus says to love your neighbor as yourself. How can you do that using your abilities and gifts? For example: treat all people I meet with respect; listen to them.

CHARTING YOUR FUTURE

LESSON 3

The future is unknown to all of us. To some, that "unknownness" seems exciting. To others it's frightening.

Because of the different problems facing our world today, teenagers sometimes worry about the future. But it's exciting to know that the Creator of the universe is interested in us and what we'll be doing in the future! And that knowledge can change the way senior highers look at their lives.

LESSON AIM

To show teenagers that God is interested in their future and can help them as they follow him.

OBJECTIVES

Students will:
● play a game and think about future occupations;
● act out Bible passages that show God is interested in our future;
● chart their goals for five, 10 and 15 years from now; and
● list one thing they'd like to be remembered for.

BIBLE BASIS

PROVERBS 3:5-6
PROVERBS 16:3-4a
ISAIAH 41:10

Look up the following scriptures. Then read the background paragraphs to see how the passages relate to your senior highers.

In **Proverbs 3:5-6**, we read that God will guide us if we trust in him.

This passage gives an exciting message to all people: If we depend on God instead of our own knowledge, he'll help us succeed. That success may not be how our world thinks of success, but we can trust God to give us what he knows is best for us.

People today tend to depend on their intellect and hard

work to help them succeed. But adults and teenagers alike can discover that depending on God will provide a much happier and more fulfilled life.

In **Proverbs 16:3-4a**, we read that everything works out the way God wants it to.

This passage echoes Proverbs 3:5-6 in some ways, but it adds a different element. If we depend on the Lord in all we do, we can reach God's idea of success—since God makes things work out the way he wants them.

For kids in an uncertain world, this truth gives a solid base. God's way is always best for us—even when we might not think so. God sees the total picture. God is our creator; he loves us and he promises to help us succeed according to his will. What more could anyone ask?

In **Isaiah 41:10**, God promises to support us.

As Christians, it's great to know we have God's help. Not only does he promise us great things, but he also promises to be with us in tough times. This passage gives us assurance that even when things look difficult, God is with us. We can lean on his strength when we're too weak to stand alone.

It's hard sometimes for kids to decide to follow God's will for their lives. They may be criticized or made fun of for the stands they take. But this passage lets them know they'll never be alone. Even if everyone else deserts them, God will still be there.

THIS LESSON AT A GLANCE

Section	Minutes	What Students Will Do	Supplies
Opener (Option 1)	5 to 10	**Occupation Connections**—Play a game, and talk about the occupation they're awarded.	Construction paper, scissors, bowl
(Option 2)		**Future Shock**—Describe what others in their group will be doing in 10 years.	Newsprint, markers
Action and Reflection	10 to 15	**Into the Future**—Write what they'd like to be doing in the future.	"Charting Your Future" handouts (p. 33), pencils
Bible Application	10 to 15	**Passage Performance**—Act out the message of Bible passages.	Bibles
Commitment	5 to 10	**Please Remember**—Tie a ribbon around a finger and say one thing they want to be remembered for.	Ribbon or yarn, "Charting Your Future" handouts from Into the Future, Bible
Closing (Option 1)	up to 5	**Travelogue to the Future**—Write a description of their partner's future.	Paper, pencils
(Option 2)		**I See**—Look through "future glasses" and suggest a neighbor's future.	Decorated eye- or sunglasses

The Lesson

OPTION 1: OCCUPATION CONNECTIONS

Before class, cut red, yellow and blue construction paper into 1×1-inch squares. Cut enough that each person can have five different-color squares. Mix all the squares in a bowl.

As kids enter, have them each grab five squares. Tell them each color has a particular value, but don't say what the value is. Allow a few minutes for kids to trade squares if they want to. Then announce the values of the various colors and have kids total their squares' value.

Say: **Your future occupations are dependent on your total scores. If you have five points or fewer, you'll be a French chef. If you have six to 10 points, you'll be the President of the United States. If you have 11 to 15 points, you'll be a missionary to the North Pole. If you have 16 to 20 points, you'll be an elephant trainer in the circus. And if you have 21 to 25 points, you'll be an elementary school principal.**

Have teenagers each tell the occupation they were assigned and explain what a "typical day on the job is like" for that occupation.

Then ask:

● **Do you like the occupation you were assigned? Why or why not?** (Yes, I've always wanted to go to the North Pole; no, I'd hate being the President.)

● **Is this a good way to decide your future?** (No, it doesn't give any choice; no, it doesn't take our abilities into account.)

Say: **We all have ideas about what we want to be in the future. Some of those ideas may change as we get older, but some may stay the same. The future is interesting to us—we have no way of knowing exactly what it holds. But we do know that God is interested in our future too. And today we'll see how he can help find what's best for us.**

OPTION 2: FUTURE SHOCK

Form groups of no more than four. Give each group a sheet of newsprint and a marker. Say: **Close your eyes. Imagine for a moment that we're able to travel through time. When I'm done talking, you'll all be transported 10 years into the future. When you get there, your job is to use the newsprint to compile a master directory of all the people in your group—and in another group if you have time. In that directory, you're to list where each person lives,**

Points for Colors
Yellow=5 points
Blue=3 points
Red=1 point

what his or her family makeup is and what he or she is doing for a career. **You may not write your own entry, someone else must write it for you. And you may not tell anyone what to write for your entry. When I call time, you'll be transported back to the present along with your directory.**

Have kids open their eyes and allow groups four to five minutes to compile their directories. Then call time. Have groups each read their directories aloud for everyone else to enjoy.

Ask:

● **Was your master directory entry something you'd really like for your future? Explain.**

● **Would you feel comfortable having someone else choose your future for you? Explain.** (No, I want to do something I like; no, I wouldn't trust someone else's judgment.)

Say: **We all have some idea of what the future holds for us or at least what we'd like to have happen. What others see us doing may not be what we think we'll be doing. The future is interesting to us. And though no one really knows exactly what it holds, we do know that God is interested in our future too. And today we'll see how he'll help us find what's best for us.**

ACTION AND REFLECTION
(10 to 15 minutes)

INTO THE FUTURE

Say: **First let's take a look at what we think we'd like to do in the future.**

Pass out the "Charting Your Future" handouts (p. 33) and pencils. Have kids each follow the instructions on their handout to map out what they'd like to see in their future.

When kids finish, form groups of no more than four. Have kids each share what they put on their chart and why. Then say: **Let's take a look at some scripture to see what God has to say about our future.**

BIBLE APPLICATION
(10 to 15 minutes)

PASSAGE PERFORMANCE

Form three groups and assign each group one of these passages: Proverbs 3:5-6; Proverbs 16:3-4a; and Isaiah 41:10. Have groups each come up with a creative way to act out the principle in their passage. One person can read the passage while the rest of the group acts it out. For example:

● Isaiah 41:10—One person could hold his or her right hand while all others kneel and look up prayerfully.

● Proverbs 3:5-6—All kids could jog in mass confusion, then line up straight upon hearing the words, "make your paths straight."

● Proverbs 16:3-4a—Group members could act out various professions: construction worker, doctor, athlete.

When groups have finished their presentations, ask:

● **How do these passages relate to God's will for our future?** (We know that God cares and will help us; if we trust God he'll make things better for us; God will work things out for the best.)

● **What help is it to us to know about these scriptures?** (We can trust that God will help us; we don't have to worry about the future because we know that God is in control.)

● **How should we as Christians approach the future differently than non-Christians?** (We shouldn't be worried about stepping on other people to climb the ladder; we should care more about what God wants and less about what will make us the most money.)

Say: **We're fortunate that God does care about our future. Because of him we have a lot less to worry about. He's our loving God, and we can know that he'll lead us into what's best for us if we follow him.**

PLEASE REMEMBER

Have kids sit in a circle. Give kids each a piece of ribbon or yarn, and have them tie it around the finger of the person sitting to their right—not tying it too tightly. Have kids do the tying one at a time, going around the circle. As each ribbon or yarn is tied, have the person tying it tell what they most want to be remembered for—their answer to the last question on the "Charting Your Future" handout from Into the Future.

Then ask:

● **How do the goals you put on the chart line up with what you think God might want you to do? Explain.**

● **Why are we sometimes afraid of what we think God might want for us in the future?** (We're afraid he might want us to do something hard, such as be a missionary; we don't think he'd want us to do something we'd enjoy.)

Read aloud Luke 12:22-31.

Ask:

● **What should be our most important goal related to our future?** (Seeking God's kingdom; pleasing God.)

● **According to Luke 12:22-31, what does God promise us if we seek him first?** (He'll give us everything we need; he'll take care of us like he cares for the rest of creation.)

Encourage kids each to commit themselves to seeking God's will first as they plan for their future.

OPTION 1: TRAVELOGUE TO THE FUTURE

Give each student a piece of paper and a pencil. Form pairs, and have the pairs write and complete the following statement for each other: "_____ (name of partner), in your future I see you _____. May God bless you in your future. In Christian love, _____ (signature).

Close by praying that God will guide your kids into his best will for each one of them.

COMMITMENT
(5 to 10 minutes)

CLOSING
(up to 5 minutes)

OPTION 2: I SEE

Before class, create a pair of "future glasses." Use an old pair of eyeglasses or sunglasses and remove the lenses. Then decorate them wildly.

Have kids stand in a circle. Then have them each take turns wearing the future glasses, looking at the person on their left and saying, "Because of God's work in your life, I see in your future . . ." Have kids complete the statement seriously and positively. Go around the circle until everyone has had a chance to wear the glasses.

If You Still Have Time . . .

Charting a New Future—Use the "Charting Your Future" handouts to help kids chart what they think God would want them to be doing at each interval. Encourage kids to keep these charts and refer to them often.

Deeper Study—Have kids use a concordance to find other scriptures on God's guidance. Have them look up words like guide, help, follow, plan, seek and find.

CHARTING

YOUR FUTURE

What would you like to be doing in your future? Will you start a family? Where will you work? Will you own a company? travel to exotic places? be a pastor or missionary?

On this map, write in things you think you'd like to be doing around each time interval.

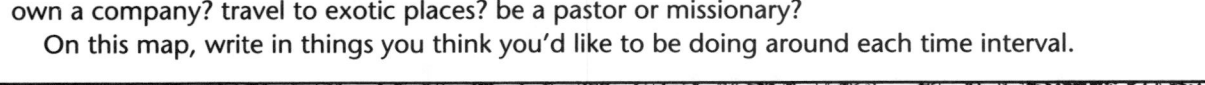

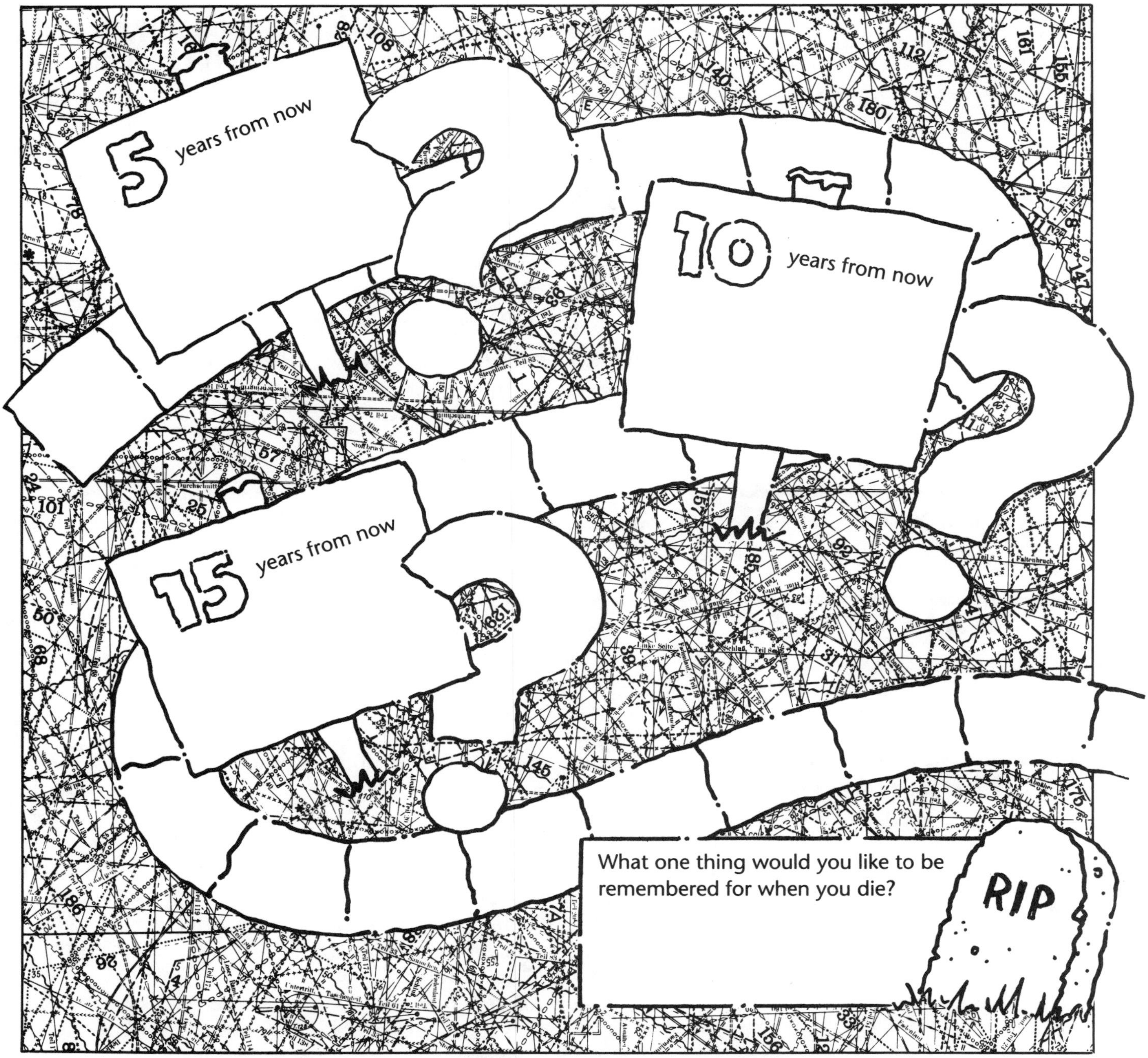

5 years from now

10 years from now

15 years from now

What one thing would you like to be remembered for when you die?

RIP

LESSON 4

WHEN YOU'VE MESSED UP

We all mess up. We make mistakes; we have accidents; we sometimes choose willfully to do wrong. And sometimes we carry a lot of guilt.

Christian teenagers are no different. They may feel guilt for something they did a month ago. Or they may feel guilt for something that really wasn't wrong. Kids can seek God's forgiveness and live their lives free of guilt's oppression. And kids can move on to reach ever higher goals as they seek to follow God's will.

LESSON AIM

To help kids accept God's forgiveness when they've messed up.

OBJECTIVES

Students will:
● experience or discuss messing up;
● act out the parable of the prodigal son; and
● celebrate God's forgiveness.

BIBLE BASIS

LUKE 15:11-32
PHILIPPIANS 3:13

Look up the following scriptures. Then read the background paragraphs to see how the passages relate to your senior highers.

In **Luke 15:11-32**, Jesus tells the story of the prodigal son. This parable gives us insight into God's forgiveness. Not only is he willing to forgive us when we sin, but he's watching and waiting for us to return to him so he can restore us to a full relationship with him.

It's easy for kids today to think of God as someone who's waiting to club them with a 2×4 if they step out of line. But God doesn't carry a 2×4, he carries a great love for each of us.

He loves us so much he sent his son to die to save us. Kids need to know that God waits patiently for them to seek his forgiveness when they've turned away from him.

In **Philippians 3:13**, Paul encourages us to look to what lies ahead.

In this passage, Paul points out he's not perfect. He still makes mistakes. But he doesn't dwell on those mistakes—instead he puts them behind him and looks to the future. He begins again to seek God's will.

Your senior highers don't have to feel guilty or unworthy of God's love because they sin. They can deal with sin the way Paul did. They can realize they're not perfect, ask God to forgive them when they sin and move on—striving toward the goal. Striving toward the goal means learning from past mistakes to keep improving, but God will always be there to offer forgiveness when kids sin.

THIS LESSON AT A GLANCE

Section	Minutes	What Students Will Do	Supplies
Opener (Option 1)	up to 5	**Tricky Trivia**—Play a game that will show them how it feels to mess up.	Question cards from a trivia game
(Option 2)		**Past Mistakes**—Tell about times they've really messed up.	
Action and Reflection	10 to 15	**When We Need Forgiveness**—Choose which actions are sins and which are mistakes.	
Bible Application	10 to 15	**The Prodigal**—Act out the story of the prodigal son.	Bibles
Commitment	10 to 15	**Coming Home**—See how their lives are like the prodigal son's.	"I Was a Prodigal Teenager" handouts (p. 40), pencils, paper with writing on one side
Closing (Option 1)	5 to 10	**Serenity Prayer**—Read a prayer and celebrate forgiveness.	Copies of "Serenity Prayer" box (p. 39), refreshments
(Option 2)		**Returned Prodigal Banquet**—Have refreshments and celebrate God's forgiveness.	Refreshments, cassette player and cassettes (optional)

The Lesson

OPTION 1: TRICKY TRIVIA

Form two teams. Form more teams if you have a large group. Tell teenagers you'll give prizes to the team that can answer five questions without a mistake. First read three easy questions to each team from a general trivia or Bible trivia game. Then read two very difficult questions to each team. Be sure at least one question for each team is too difficult for anyone to answer.

Then ask:

● **How did you feel after you'd answered the first questions correctly?** (Great, I thought we were going to make it; nervous, I was afraid we'd miss one.)

● **How did you feel when you messed up?** (Terrible; not so bad; frustrated.)

● **How do you feel when you do things you know are displeasing to God?** (Lousy; uneasy; angry.)

Say: **We all mess up from time to time. Sometimes we make mistakes on little things like this trivia game. Other times we mess up in big ways when we do things we know are wrong. And we often feel terrible. Today we're going to look at how to deal with those feelings and mistakes.**

OPTION 2: PAST MISTAKES

Ask for volunteers to tell about times they've really messed up on something. Have a story of your own ready to tell to get the sharing started. After several have told of times they've messed up, ask:

● **How did you feel when you messed up?** (Terrible; not so bad; frustrated.)

● **How do you feel when you do things you know are displeasing to God?** (Lousy; uneasy; angry.)

Say: **We all mess up from time to time. Sometimes we make mistakes on little things. Other times we mess up in big ways when we do things we know are wrong. And we often feel terrible. Today we're going to look at how to deal with those feelings and mistakes.**

WHEN WE NEED FORGIVENESS

Ask:

● **What's the difference between something that's just a mistake and something that's wrong?** (A mistake is just an accident; something that's wrong is something that makes God angry.)

● **What should we do to right a simple mistake?** (Just figure out what we did wrong; try not to do it again.)

● **What should we do to right something we've done wrong?** (Admit we've sinned; ask God for forgiveness; try not to do it again.)

Designate one end of your room as "mistake" and the other end as "sin." As you read each of the questions from the box in the margin, have your kids stand at the end of the room that matches what they think the description describes. If kids aren't all at one end, have the kids at opposite ends briefly debate the issue.

When you've gone through all the descriptions, ask:

● **How do sins take us away from doing God's will?** (Sins aren't God's will; they focus on what we want, not what God wants.)

● **Can you mess up even when you're actively seeking to do God's will? Explain.** (Yes, we're not perfect; sure, we don't always know his will that well; it's easy to make a wrong decision.)

● **Is it easy to "turn around" from your sin and seek God's will again? Why or why not?** (Yes, I know when I've blown it and I want to do what's right; no, pride makes it tough to admit when you're wrong.)

Say: **When we sin we need to ask God for forgiveness. And asking that forgiveness helps us get back on track with doing God's will.**

Mistake or Sin?

● You used a pen on the counter at the bank and later realized you had it with you in the car.

● Your little brother kept pestering you until you yelled at him and told him you never wanted to see him again.

● Your dad gave you $10 to buy a gift for your mom. You stuck it in your wallet, forgot what it was for and later spent it on a pizza.

● Your family's income was cut off because of illness, and you decided to swipe an expensive vase from a friend's house to sell it and buy food.

● You were finished with your history test and just glancing around the room when you noticed a good student had marked an answer differently. So you changed yours.

● You left a ball lying on your front steps, knowing it was dangerous. A good friend stepped on it, fell and sprained her ankle.

THE PRODIGAL

Have your kids act out the story of the prodigal son from Luke 15:11-32. Choose senior highers to play the parts of the father, the older son, the younger son and the narrator.

Ask the narrator to read the scripture passage aloud while the characters act out their parts. Have the narrator pause after each verse and have the rest of the kids in the class repeat the last two words of the verse for emphasis. For example, when the narrator reads "There was a man who had two sons," the group should respond, "two sons."

After the performance, ask:

● **How is this story like times we sin?** (Sometimes we take advantage of God; God wants us to come back to him; God is just waiting to forgive us.)

● **How is God like the father in the story?** (He's patient; he lets us sin if we choose to; he loves us enough to forgive us.)

● **What makes it hard to return to God and ask for forgiveness when we've sinned?** (We're too proud; we don't

---

BIBLE APPLICATION
(10 to 15 minutes)

really want to stop sinning; we're afraid he won't want us anymore.)

Say: **God has promised to forgive us if we turn from our sin and ask him to forgive us. We don't have to worry that we've done something too bad for God to forgive. He'll be there waiting when we return to him.**

COMMITMENT
(10 to 15 minutes)

COMING HOME

Pass out the "I Was a Prodigal Teenager" handouts (p. 40) and pencils. Have kids answer the questions individually.

When kids are finished with their handouts, allow volunteers to share what they've written, but don't force anyone to speak.

Then say: **Here's a formula for dealing with sin: Confess it and ask for forgiveness; accept God's forgiveness; learn from what you did wrong; and seek God's will once again. When God forgives a sin, he forgets it—and we should put it behind us too.**

Have kids each stand and face the same direction. Hold up a sheet of paper with lots of words written on it for them to see. Ask them to imagine that the words on the paper describe times they've gone against God's will. Then have them each turn around in a full circle and face the same spot again. As they're turning, flip the paper to reveal the blank side.

Say: **Just as the words on this paper were replaced by a blank sheet, your sins can be erased and replaced with a "clean slate" on which you can plan how you'll seek God's will for your life.**

CLOSING
(5 to 10 minutes)

OPTION 1: SERENITY PRAYER

Photocopy the "Serenity Prayer" box (p. 39). Pass out copies to your kids. Say: **Most of us have seen the first part of this prayer, but few have probably seen the rest. It provides a good look at one man's understanding of God's will. It may give all of us insights into how we can follow that will.**

Read the prayer aloud together.

To wrap up this class and this study, share refreshments of some kind, and celebrate together God's forgiveness and the desire to do his will.

OPTION 2: RETURNED PRODIGAL BANQUET

Have a minibanquet celebrating God's forgiveness. Bring refreshments, eat and be merry!

If your group sings, sing praise songs and choruses. Or play uplifting contemporary Christian music such as "Great is the Lord" by Michael W. Smith from the *Michael W. Smith*

Project (Word) or "Awesome God" by Rich Mullins from *Winds of Heaven—Stuff of Earth* (Word).

Close your class with a joyous prayer of thanks to God for his forgiveness and guidance in our lives.

Serenity Prayer

God,
grant me the serenity to
accept the things I cannot change,
courage to change the things I can, and
wisdom to know the difference,
living one day at a time,
enjoying one moment at a time,
accepting hardship as a pathway to peace,
taking as Jesus did,
this sinful world as it is,
not as I would have it,
trusting that you will
make all things right
if I surrender to your will,
so that I may be reasonably happy
in this life and supremely happy with you
forever in the next.
—*Reinhold Niebuhr*

If You Still Have Time . . .

Modern Prodigal—Have your kids rewrite the parable of the prodigal son into a modern situation. You might want to put the parable in a church newsletter or have the kids act it out for the whole congregation.

Course Reflection—Form a circle. Ask students to reflect on the past four lessons. Have them take turns completing the following sentences:

- Something I learned in this course was . . .
- If I could tell my friends about this course, I'd say . . .
- Something I'll do differently because of this course is . . .

I WAS A PRODIGAL TEENAGER

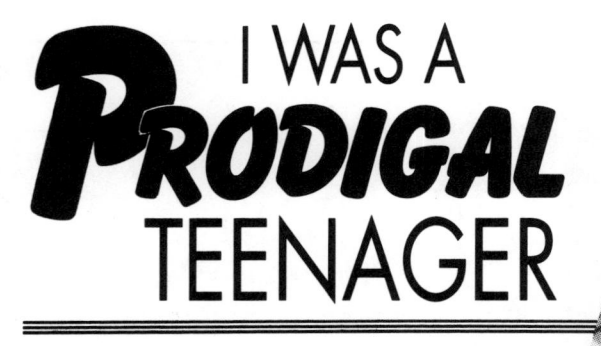

Write your answers to the following questions in the space provided.

1. How are you like the prodigal son? Describe a time you really messed up with God.

2. Think of a time you've experienced forgiveness like the prodigal son did. How did you feel?

3. Have you ever felt like the older brother? If so, what did you do about those feelings?

4. What is the best thing to do when you realize you've sinned? Why isn't it always easy to do?

5. Read 1 John 1:9. What is God's promise related to forgiveness?

6. Read Philippians 3:13. What does God want us to do after he grants us forgiveness for something we've done wrong?

7. How can you redirect and seek God's will after you've messed up?

BONUS IDEAS

Cheer On!—Have kids make pennants to cheer themselves on to follow God's will for their lives. Have kids each make a pennant and write on it future goals and ambitions they feel are in line with God's will for their lives. Encourage kids each to hang their pennant in their room as a reminder to always seek God's will in pursuing their goals.

Kill the Fatted Calf—Have your kids plan and hold a Prodigal Son Banquet for your whole church. Have kids serve the dinner, then put on a dramatic production of the prodigal son parable set in modern times. Or have kids perform the parable with puppets.

It's a Wonderful Life—This classic movie, *It's a Wonderful Life*, makes a powerful case for how one life can make a lot of difference in the world. And there are conversations among angels that raise interesting questions of God's will. The movie is in the public domain, which means you can show it to a group without worrying about violating copyright.

Digging Into God's Will—Dig deeper into the topic of discovering God's will for your future by leading your kids through a study of one of the following booklets: "Affirming the Will of God" by Paul Little (InterVarsity Press); "Finding God's Will" by J.I. Packer (InterVarsity Press); or "God's Will" by Charles R. Swindoll (Multnomah Press).

Working It Through—Use the "Decisions, Decisions" handout (p. 43) to help kids work through a decision-making process that can help them discern God's will. When you're finished, give kids extra copies of the handout to use in working through decisions in the future.

The Lost Coin—Lead your senior highers in a study of the parable of the lost coin (Luke 15:8-10). Draw a parallel between the search for the coin and the search for God's will. Discuss the importance of seeking God's will in everything we do.

Game-O-Rama—Use the God's Will Game-O-Rama activities from *GROUP Magazine's Best Youth Group Programs* (Group Books) to have some fun with learning how to discover God's will.

Chariots of Fire—Show the movie *Chariots of Fire* to your

MEETINGS AND MORE

BONUS SCRIPTURES

The lessons focus on a select few scripture passages, but if you'd like to incorporate more Bible readings into the lessons, here are our suggestions:

- Nehemiah 9:17 (God is ready to pardon; he is gracious and merciful.)
- Psalm 143:8-10 (The psalmist asks God to teach him to do God's will.)
- Micah 7:18-19 (God has compassion on us.)
- Mark 9:20-23 (All things are possible for those who believe.)
- John 8:12 (If we follow God we will not walk in darkness.)
- Philippians 2:12-13 (God creates the desire in us to work for his good pleasure.)

kids. This movie's main character makes major decisions based on what he thinks is God's will for him. Stop the film at tough decision points and work through the decisions with your kids. At the end, evaluate the decisions made by all the main characters. Which decisions seemed to be in line with God's will and which decisions didn't? Be sure to get permission to show the movie to your group. For permission and group rental information, contact Films, Inc., 5547 N. Ravenswood, Chicago, IL 60640, 1-800-323-4222.

Obeying God's Will—Sometimes it's harder to obey God's will than to find it. Lead your kids in a study of John 14:15-24. Discuss why it's important to obey the parts of God's will we're sure about. Point out that obeying the things we're sure about may help us avoid some of the problems we're not so sure about.

Table Talk—Use the Table Talk handout (p. 19) to build a meeting for parents and kids. Open the meeting with fun crowdbreakers. For crowdbreaker ideas, check out *Quick Crowdbreakers and Games for Youth Groups* (Group Books). Provide refreshments and let kids work through the handouts with their parents. Take advantage of the time together to discuss the topic of finding God's will with kids and parents. Have parents tell stories of ways God has guided them in the past.

RETREAT IDEA

Facing the Future Together—Build a retreat around the theme of seeking God's will for the future. Include teenagers and their parents—or substitute parents. Vary the activities in the retreat to include time for teenagers alone, time for parents alone, time for teenagers to work through questions with their parents and time for teenagers to work through questions with other kids' parents.

Have kids and parents each complete the "Decisions, Decisions" handout (p. 43) for one of the activities.

Be sure to celebrate all the good things that happen.

PARTY PLEASER

The-Future-Is-Now Party—Have a full-blown future party. Have everyone come dressed as they'd like to be 10 years from now. Talk about favorite church and Sunday school memories as if you were looking back on them 10 years from now. Serve wild refreshments like you think might be served in the future.

DECISIONS, DECISIONS

Use this worksheet to help you work through tough decisions. Work through the steps one at a time, then examine all you've written to help you decide.

1. Pray for God's guidance through the decision process. Don't make this a one-step thing; pray through all the steps, asking God to help you decide.

2. List all the options. Don't rule anything out. Try to think of at least three. Then write the good things and the bad things about each option.

Option:

   Why it's good: Why it's bad:

Option:

   Why it's good: Why it's bad:

Option:

   Why it's good: Why it's bad:

3. Write the consequences of each option—for you, for your family, for your friends, for anyone else involved.

4. Find three passages of scripture that apply to your situation. Write what it seems those passages would have you do.

Passage A:

Passage B:

Passage C:

5. Seek advice from other people: your parents, your friends, your pastor or youth worker, another adult you respect. Think about which option most people in your church would choose. Be sure you talk to someone at least 10 years older than you. Write what each person says.

6. Based on all the information on this sheet, rule out any innapropriate options. Then carefully examine the remaining options and prayerfully choose the one that seems best.

CURRICULUM REORDER—TOP PRIORITY

Order now to prepare for your upcoming Sunday school classes, youth ministry meetings, and weekend retreats! Each book includes all teacher and student materials—plus photocopiable handouts—for any size class . . . for just $7.99 each!

FOR SENIOR HIGH:

1 & 2 Corinthians: Christian Discipleship, ISBN 1-55945-230-7

Changing the World, ISBN 1-55945-236-6

Christians in a Non-Christian World, ISBN 1-55945-224-2

Christlike Leadership, ISBN 1-55945-231-5

Communicating With Friends, ISBN 1-55945-228-5

Counterfeit Religions, ISBN 1-55945-207-2

Dating Decisions, ISBN 1-55945-215-3

Deciphering Jesus' Parables, ISBN 1-55945-237-4

Exodus: Following God, ISBN 1-55945-226-9

Exploring Ethical Issues, ISBN 1-55945-225-0

Faith for Tough Times, ISBN 1-55945-216-1

Forgiveness, ISBN 1-55945-223-4

Getting Along With Parents, ISBN 1-55945-202-1

Getting Along With Your Family, ISBN 1-55945-233-1

The Gospel of John: Jesus' Teachings, ISBN 1-55945-208-0

Hazardous to Your Health: AIDS, Steroids & Eating Disorders, ISBN 1-55945-200-5

Is Marriage in Your Future?, ISBN 1-55945-203-X

Jesus' Death & Resurrection, ISBN 1-55945-211-0

The Joy of Serving, ISBN 1-55945-210-2

Knowing God's Will, ISBN 1-55945-205-6

Life After High School, ISBN 1-55945-220-X

Making Good Decisions, ISBN 1-55945-209-9

Money: A Christian Perspective, ISBN 1-55945-212-9

Movies, Music, TV & Me, ISBN 1-55945-213-7

Overcoming Insecurities, ISBN 1-55945-221-8

Responding to Injustice, ISBN 1-55945-214-5

Revelation, ISBN 1-55945-229-3

School Struggles, ISBN 1-55945-201-3

Sex: A Christian Perspective, ISBN 1-55945-206-4

Today's Lessons From Yesterday's Prophets, ISBN 1-55945-227-7

Turning Depression Upside Down, ISBN 1-55945-135-1

What Is the Church?, ISBN 1-55945-222-6

Who Is God?, ISBN 1-55945-218-8

Who Is Jesus?, ISBN 1-55945-219-6

Who Is the Holy Spirit?, ISBN 1-55945-217-X

Your Life as a Disciple, ISBN 1-55945-204-8

FOR JUNIOR HIGH/MIDDLE SCHOOL:

Accepting Others: Beyond Barriers & Stereotypes, ISBN 1-55945-126-2

Advice to Young Christians: Exploring Paul's Letters, ISBN 1-55945-146-7

Applying the Bible to Life, ISBN 1-55945-116-5

Becoming Responsible, ISBN 1-55945-109-2

Bible Heroes: Joseph, Esther, Mary & Peter, ISBN 1-55945-137-8

Boosting Self-Esteem, ISBN 1-55945-100-9

Building Better Friendships, ISBN 1-55945-138-6

Can Christians Have Fun?, ISBN 1-55945-134-3

Caring for God's Creation, ISBN 1-55945-121-1

Christmas: A Fresh Look, ISBN 1-55945-124-6

Competition, ISBN 1-55945-133-5

Dealing With Death, ISBN 1-55945-112-2

Dealing With Disappointment, ISBN 1-55945-139-4

Drugs & Drinking, ISBN 1-55945-118-1

Evil and the Occult, ISBN 1-55945-102-5

Genesis: The Beginnings, ISBN 1-55945-111-4

Guys & Girls: Understanding Each Other, ISBN 1-55945-110-6

Handling Conflict, ISBN 1-55945-125-4

Heaven & Hell, ISBN 1-55945-131-9

Is God Unfair?, ISBN 1-55945-108-4

Love or Infatuation?, ISBN 1-55945-128-9

Making Parents Proud, ISBN 1-55945-107-6

Making the Most of School, ISBN 1-55945-113-0

Materialism, ISBN 1-55945-130-0

Miracles!, ISBN 1-55945-117-3

Peace & War, ISBN 1-55945-123-8

Peer Pressure, ISBN 1-55945-103-3

Prayer, ISBN 1-55945-104-1

Reaching Out to a Hurting World, ISBN 1-55945-140-8

Sermon on the Mount, ISBN 1-55945-129-7

Suicide: The Silent Epidemic, ISBN 1-55945-145-9

Telling Your Friends About Christ, ISBN 1-55945-114-9

The Ten Commandments, ISBN 1-55945-127-0

Today's Music: Good or Bad?, ISBN 1-55945-101-7

What Is God's Purpose for Me?, ISBN 1-55945-132-7

What's a Christian?, ISBN 1-55945-105-X

Order today from your local Christian bookstore, or write: Group Publishing, Box 485, Loveland, CO 80539. For mail orders, please add postage/handling of $4 for orders up to $15, $5 for orders of $15.01+. Colorado residents add 3% sales tax.

Blast away boredom with these upcoming scripture-based topics.

For Senior High:

- Dating
- Making decisions
- Materialism

- New Age
- Being a servant
- Injustice

- Who is God?
- Music and media
- Faith in tough times

For Junior High:

- Success in school
- Independence
- Body-health

- Miracles
- Relationships: Guys and girls
- Sharing faith

- Handling conflict
- Creation
- The Bible

For more details write:

Box 481 ● Loveland, CO 80539 ● 800-747-6060

BRING THE BIBLE TO LIFE FOR YOUR 5TH- AND 6TH-GRADERS WITH GROUP'S *HANDS-ON BIBLE CURRICULUM™*

Energize your kids with Active Learning!

Group's **Hands-On Bible Curriculum™** will help you teach the Bible in a radical new way. It's based on Active Learning—the same teaching method Jesus used.

Research shows that we retain less than 10% of what we hear or read. *But we remember up to 90% of what we experience.* Your 5th- and 6th-graders will experience spiritual lessons and learn to apply them to their daily lives! And—they'll go home remembering what they've learned.

In each lesson, students will participate in exciting and memorable learning experiences using fascinating gadgets and gizmos you've not seen with any other curriculum. Your 5th- and 6th-graders will discover biblical truths and <u>remember</u> what they learn—because they're <u>doing</u> instead of just listening.

You'll save time and money too!

While students are learning more, you'll be working less—simply follow the quick and easy instructions in the **Teachers Guide**. You'll get tons of material for an energy-packed 35- to 60-minute lesson. And, if you have extra time, there's an arsenal of Bonus Ideas and Time Stuffers to keep kids occupied—and learning! Plus, you'll SAVE BIG over other curriculum programs that require you to buy expensive separate student books—all student handouts in Group's **Hands-On Bible Curriculum™** are photocopiable!

In addition to the easy-to-use **Teachers Guide**, you'll get all the essential teaching materials you need in a ready-to-use **Learning Lab™**. No more running from store to store hunting for lesson materials—all the active-learning tools you need to teach 13 exciting Bible lessons to any size class are provided for you in the **Learning Lab™**.

Challenging topics every 13 weeks keep your kids coming back!

Group's **Hands-On Bible Curriculum™** covers topics that matter to your kids and teaches them the Bible with integrity. Every quarter you'll explore three meaningful subjects. One is centered around learning about <u>others</u>...another helps your students learn about <u>themselves</u>...and a third teaches your kids about <u>God</u>. Switching topics every month keeps your 5th- and 6th-graders enthused and coming back for more. The full 2-year program will help your kids...

- make God-pleasing decisions,
- recognize their God-given potential, and
- seek to grow as Christians.

Take the boredom out of Sunday school, children's church, and youth group for your 5th- and 6th-graders. Make your job easier and more rewarding with no-fail lessons that are ready in a flash. Order Group's **Hands-On Bible Curriculum™** for your 5th- and 6th-graders today.

QUARTER 1, YEAR B
Teachers Guide	ISBN 1-55945-314-1	$14.99
Learning Lab™	ISBN 1-55945-315-X	$34.99

QUARTER 2, YEAR B
Teachers Guide	ISBN 1-55945-316-8	$14.99
Learning Lab™	ISBN 1-55945-317-6	$34.99

Order today from your local Christian bookstore, or write: Group Publishing, Box 485, Loveland, CO 80539. For mail orders, please add postage/handling of $4 for orders up to $15, $5 for orders of $15.01+. Colorado residents add 3% sales tax.